Animal Top Tens

Africa's Most Amazing Animals

Anita Ganeri

Raintree is an imprint of Capstone Global Library Limited, a company incorporated in England and Wales having its registered office at 7 Pilgrim Street, London, EC4V 6LB – Registered company number: 6695582

"Raintree" is a registered trademark of Pearson Education Limited, under licence to Capstone Global Library Limited

Text © Capstone Global Library Limited 2008
First published in hardback in 2008
Paperback edition first published in 2009

Editorial: Nancy Dickmann and Catherine Veitch
Design: Victoria Bevan and Geoff Ward
Illustrations: Geoff Ward
Picture Research: Mica Brancic
Production: Victoria Fitzgerald

Originated by Modern Age
Printed and bound by CTPS (China Translation & Printing Services Ltd)

13-digit ISBN 978 1 4062 0914 3 (hardback)
12 11 10 09 08
10 9 8 7 6 5 4 3 2 1

13-digit ISBN 978 1 4062 0924 2 (paperback)
13 12 11 10 09
10 9 8 7 6 5 4 3 2 1

British Library Cataloguing in Publication Data
Ganeri, Anita, 1961-
Africa's Most Amazing Animals.
(Animal top tens)
591.9'6
A full catalogue record for this book is available from the British Library.

Acknowledgements
The author and publisher are grateful to the following for permission to reproduce copyright material: ©Ardea pp. **8** (Chris Harvey), **10** (M. Watson), **18** (Pat Morris); ©FLPA pp. **4** (Ariadne Van Zandbergen), **7** (Ariadne Van Zandbergen) [Ardea], **19** (David Hosking), **27** (Fritz Polking); ©FLPA/Minden Pictures pp. **20**, **23**; ©Naturepl pp. **13** (Bruce Davidson); ©NHPA p. **21** (Stephen Dalton); ©OSF pp. **6** (Francois Savigny), **9** (Tom Brakefield), **11** (Karl Ammann), **14** (Gallo Images-Anthony Bannister), **15** (Austin J. Stevens), **16**, **17** (Dupc Dupc/David Haring), **22** (Roger De La Harpe), **24** (Patti Murray), **26** (Wisniewski Wisniewski).

Cover photograph of an aye-aye, reproduced with permission of OSF/David Haring/Dupc.

The publishers would like to thank Michael Bright for his assistance with the preparation of this book.

Contents

Some words are printed in bold, **like this**. You can find out what they mean on page 31 in the Glossary.

Africa

Africa is the world's second largest **continent**, covering about 30,000,000 sq kilometres (11,580,000 sq miles). Several islands lie off the coast, including Madagascar.

Africa has many different kinds of landscape. The Sahara Desert is in the north. It is the world's biggest desert and it covers a third of the continent. The **equator** crosses central Africa and **rainforests** grow here. To the east are rolling **grasslands**. There are also snow-capped mountains, and some of the world's longest rivers and largest lakes can be found in Africa.

The grasslands of East Africa are famous for their amazing animals.

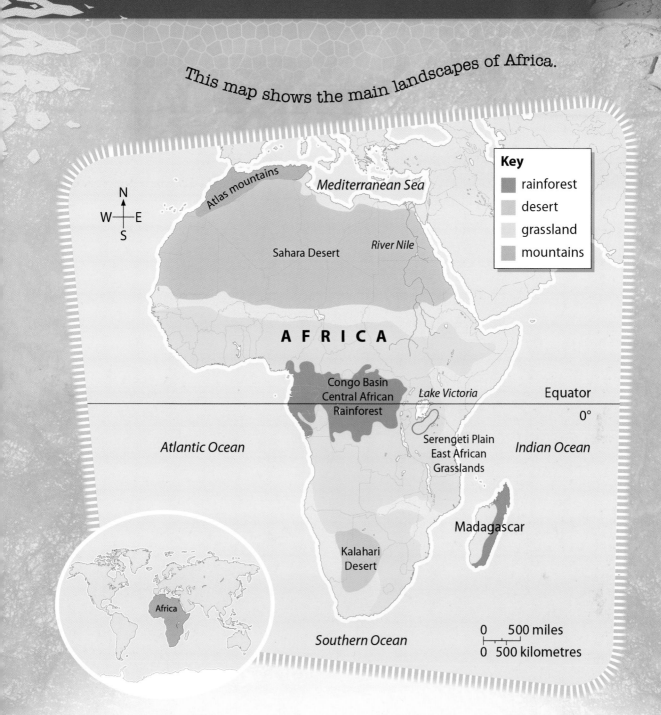

Key
- rainforest
- desert
- grassland
- mountains

Atlas mountains

Mediterranean Sea

N
W E
S

Sahara Desert

River Nile

A F R I C A

Congo Basin
Central African
Rainforest

Lake Victoria

Equator
0°

Atlantic Ocean

Serengeti Plain
East African
Grasslands

Indian Ocean

Madagascar

Africa

Kalahari
Desert

0   500 miles
0   500 kilometres

Southern Ocean

An amazing range of animals live in the different
landscapes. Huge herds of zebra and wildebeest roam
the grassy plains. Hippos and crocodiles swim in rivers
and **swamps.** Flamingos and other birds flock to the
lakes to nest and feed. Chimpanzees and gorillas live in
the rainforests. These animals have special features
to help them survive in their particular **habitats.**

Savannah elephant

The Savannah elephant is the world's largest land animal. It is a **mammal**. Its body is designed for feeding on the grasses and plants that grow in its **grassland** habitat.

Elephant food

The elephant changes what it eats when the seasons change. In the wet season it mainly eats grasses as there are plenty of them. In the dry season the grasses die. Then the elephant eats bark, twigs, flowers, fruits, and roots.

Savannah elephants use their huge ears as fans to cool down their bodies.

Body design

An elephant's skull, jaws, and teeth are able to eat hard plants. The tusks are actually very long front teeth. The elephant uses them for stripping bark from trees and digging up roots. An elephant also has large teeth inside its mouth for grinding food. An elephant's trunk is really its nose. It uses it to smell and also to pick up food.

SAVANNAH ELEPHANT

BODY LENGTH:
4–5 M (13–16 FT)

WEIGHT:
4–7 TONNES
(4.4–7.7 TONS)

LIFESPAN:
60 YEARS

HABITAT:
GRASSLAND

THAT'S AMAZING!:
AN ELEPHANT'S TUSKS GROW THROUGHOUT ITS LIFE AND CAN REACH MORE THAN 3 M (10 FT) LONG.

where savannah elephants live

Africa

Atlantic Ocean

Indian Ocean

Southern Ocean

Elephants need to eat about 150 kg (330 lbs) of food a day.

Cheetah

On the **grasslands**, cheetahs hunt animals, such as small antelopes. The cheetah starts by **stalking** its **prey**. It hides amongst the tall, dry grass. When it is close enough to its prey, it suddenly chases.

CHEETAH

BODY LENGTH:
UP TO 1.5 M (4.9 FT)

TAIL LENGTH:
UP TO 85 CM (33.1 IN)

WEIGHT:
40–65 KG (88–143 LBS)

LIFESPAN:
UP TO 12 YEARS

HABITAT:
GRASSLAND AND SEMI-DESERT

THAT'S AMAZING!:
CHEETAH CUBS SPEND MOST OF THEIR TIME PLAYING GAMES OF STALKING AND POUNCING. THIS IS A WAY OF PRACTISING FOR HUNTING WHEN THEY GROW UP.

where cheetahs live

Africa

Atlantic Ocean

Indian Ocean

Southern Ocean

A cheetah can reach a top speed of 110 kph (68.3 mph).

A cheetah can only run for a short distance before it gets tired.

Built for speed

A cheetah is the fastest animal and **mammal** on land. Its slender body is built for speed. Its bendy backbone allows it to take giant leaps. Its claws grip on the ground like spikes in a running shoe. A cheetah uses its tail for steering when it turns quickly after its prey.

Ostrich

Ostriches are the world's largest, heaviest, and tallest birds. Males have black and white feathers. Females are greyish-brown. An ostrich cannot fly but has long, powerful legs for running fast. When it is in danger, an ostrich runs away. It can move as quickly as 70 kph (43.4 mph). It also uses its legs in self-defence. It can kick and slash with its sharp claws.

OSTRICH

HEIGHT:
1.7–2.7 M
(5.7–8.8 FT)

WEIGHT:
UP TO 150 KG
(330 LBS)

LIFESPAN:
50 YEARS

HABITAT:
GRASSLANDS; DESERTS

THAT'S AMAZING!:
OSTRICHES CAN LIVE WITHOUT WATER FOR A LONG TIME. THIS IS VERY USEFUL BECAUSE THEY LIVE IN DRY PLACES. THEY GET MOISTURE FROM THE PLANTS THEY EAT.

where ostriches live

Africa

Atlantic
Ocean

Indian
Ocean

Southern Ocean

Ostriches have two toes on their feet. Their toes help them to run fast.

Swallowing stones

Ostriches spend much of the day feeding. They eat whatever they can find in their **habitat**. This means mostly plants, especially roots, leaves, and seeds. But they also eat **insects** and small lizards. Ostriches do not have teeth for chewing food so they swallow stones, pebbles, and sand to help grind up their food.

An ostrich egg is very big. It is ten times bigger than a chicken egg.

Goliath beetle

The goliath beetle is one of the biggest **insects** in the world. Adults can weigh three times as much as a mouse. Goliath beetles eat sap and fruit from **rainforest** trees.

GOLIATH BEETLE

BODY LENGTH:
UP TO 15 CM (5.8 IN)

WEIGHT:
70–100 G (2.4–3.5 OZ)

LIFESPAN:
FEW MONTHS (ADULTS)

HABITAT:
RAINFOREST

THAT'S AMAZING!:
GOLIATH BEETLES HAVE SHARP CLAWS AT THE END OF EACH LEG TO HELP THEM CLIMB TREES TO FEED.

where goliath beetles live

Africa

Atlantic Ocean

Indian Ocean

Southern Ocean

A male goliath beetle has a Y-shaped horn on its head.

Goliath beetles are so large that they make a noise like a mini-helicopter when they fly.

Beetle life cycle

The life cycle of a goliath beetle is linked to the seasons of the rainforest. The beetle lays its eggs on the forest floor early in the rainy season. When the **larvae** hatch, they feed on rotting leaves and wood. Then they burrow in the ground and build a hard case of soil around them. Inside, their bodies change into adults. They stay in the ground until the dry season ends. When the rainy season begins again, they break out of their cases and search for a **mate**.

Gaboon viper

The Gaboon viper is a large snake with brown, pink, and orange skin. It has diamond-shaped marks down its sides. This colouring gives it excellent **camouflage**. By the time the snake's **prey** spots the snake, it is too late to escape.

The snake's colouring makes it very difficult to spot on the rainforest floor.

Fangs and food

The Gaboon viper feeds on birds and small **mammals**, such as rats. It hunts for food at night. It waits for its prey to come near, then kills it with a bite. The bite is so poisonous that it can kill a small animal instantly. The viper does not only kill when it is hungry. It will also attack if it is threatened or disturbed.

where Gaboon vipers live

Africa

Atlantic Ocean

Indian Ocean

Southern Ocean

GABOON VIPER

HEIGHT:
UP TO 2 M (6.56 FT)

WEIGHT:
7–10 KG (15–22 LBS)

LIFESPAN:
15–20 YEARS (IN **CAPTIVITY**)

HABITAT:
RAINFOREST

THAT'S AMAZING!:
ONE GABOON VIPER MAKES ENOUGH **VENOM** TO KILL AT LEAST 50 MONKEYS.

The viper has the longest fangs of any snake. Its fangs can grow up to 5 cm (2 in) long.

Aye-aye

The aye-aye is a small **mammal**. It has bat-like ears, big yellow eyes, and large front teeth. Its tail is long and bushy and its thick grey-brown coat is flecked with white. It lives high up in the trees of the **rainforest**.

AYE-AYE

HEIGHT:
30–40 CM (11.7–15.6 IN)

TAIL LENGTH:
40–50 CM
(15.6–19.5 IN)

WEIGHT:
2–3 KG
(4.4–6.6 LBS)

LIFESPAN:
UP TO 23 YEARS
(IN **CAPTIVITY**)

HABITAT:
RAINFORESTS, DRY
FORESTS IN MADAGASCAR

THAT'S AMAZING!:
THE AYE-AYE SPENDS THE DAY
SLEEPING IN A NEST MADE FROM
LEAVES AND TWIGS, THEN GOES
OUT HUNTING AT NIGHT.

where aye-ayes live

Indian
Ocean

Atlantic
Ocean

Africa

Madagascar

Southern Ocean

The aye-aye's large eyes and ears help it to locate its **prey** at night.

Finger food

The aye-aye has very long, middle fingers which it uses for scooping out fruits and for finding **insect larvae.** The aye-aye taps on a tree branch and listens out for hollow spaces where larvae might be found.

Madagascar
Madagascar lies off the south-east coast of Africa and is the world's fourth largest island. It is home to some of the most unusual wildlife on Earth. About 80 per cent of its animals, including the aye-aye, are found nowhere else in the world.

The aye-aye tears the wood open with its teeth and uses its finger to pull the grubs out.

Sociable weaverbird

Sociable weaverbirds live in the dry desert. They hardly need to drink because they get moisture from the seeds and **insects** they eat.

Sociable weaverbirds are small, brown birds about the size of sparrows.

SOCIABLE WEAVERBIRD

BODY LENGTH:
14 CM (5.4 IN)

WEIGHT:
26–30 G (0.9–1 OZ)

LIFESPAN:
UP TO 5 YEARS

HABITAT:
DESERT

THAT'S AMAZING!:
A SOCIABLE WEAVERBIRD NEST CAN WEIGH SEVERAL TONNES. IT CAN GET SO HEAVY THAT IT KNOCKS DOWN THE TREE IT IS BUILT ON.

where sociable weaverbirds live

Africa

Atlantic Ocean

Indian Ocean

Southern Ocean

The roof of the nest is made from large twigs. The chambers are built from dry grasses and lined with soft leaves or fur.

Living together

Living with lots of birds has its advantages. Parents have helpers for their chicks. Weaverbirds also share their nest with other birds, such as falcons, finches, and owls. These visitors help to keep watch for danger.

Nest building

Weaverbirds build enormous nests in the trees. A single nest may have **chambers** for up to 100 families. The nest keeps the birds comfortable in the tough desert climate. On cold nights, the cosy inner chambers keep the birds warm. On hot summer days the birds stay cool in chambers on the outside of the nest.

Desert locust

The desert locust is a kind of grasshopper. It lives in the desert and feeds on plants. It eats about its own weight in food each day. The locust is usually shy and lives alone but all this changes if it starts to rain. The rain makes plants grow and this gives plenty of food for the locusts and their young. Then the locusts breed quickly and form enormous **swarms**.

Even a small swarm can contain about 50 million **insects**.

Locust swarms

The swarms of locusts can fly hundreds of kilometres a day, carried by the wind. They eat any plants they can find. A swarm of locusts can eat hundreds of thousands of tonnes (tons) of food in a day.

DESERT LOCUST

BODY LENGTH:
4.5–6 CM (1.7–2.3 IN)

WEIGHT:
2 G (0.07 OZ)

LIFESPAN:
3–5 MONTHS

HABITAT:
DESERTS

THAT'S AMAZING!:
LOCUSTS LAY UP TO 100 EGGS IN AN EGG POD IN THE SAND. THE FEMALE COVERS THEM WITH FOAMY FROTH TO STOP THE EGGS DRYING OUT.

where desert locusts live

Africa

Atlantic Ocean

Indian Ocean

Southern Ocean

Locusts destroy crops on farms.

Nile crocodile

The Nile crocodile is one of the world's largest **reptiles**. The crocodile lies in the water waiting for its **prey**. Then it grabs its victim in its huge jaws and drags it beneath the water to drown it.

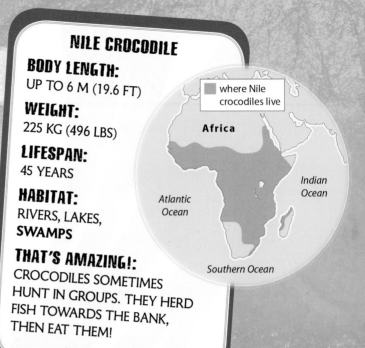

NILE CROCODILE

BODY LENGTH:
UP TO 6 M (19.6 FT)

WEIGHT:
225 KG (496 LBS)

LIFESPAN:
45 YEARS

HABITAT:
RIVERS, LAKES, **SWAMPS**

THAT'S AMAZING!:
CROCODILES SOMETIMES HUNT IN GROUPS. THEY HERD FISH TOWARDS THE BANK, THEN EAT THEM!

where Nile crocodiles live

Africa

Atlantic Ocean

Indian Ocean

Southern Ocean

A crocodile's grey-green colouring gives fantastic **camouflage**.

crocodile waiting for prey

The mother carries the babies in her mouth to the water for their first swim.

Eggs and babies

A female crocodile lays her eggs in a hole in the river bank and covers them with sand. Both parents guard the nest. When the baby crocodiles are ready to hatch, they make a chirping sound and the female digs up the eggs.

Lungfish

The lungfish is a fish with a long, snake-like body. It lives in shallow water in **swamps** and streams. Lungfish are fierce hunters and will eat anything they can catch. They mainly feed on frogs, small fish, and crabs.

gills

In the wet season, lungfish breathe oxygen from the water through their **gills**.

Out of water

In the wet season, when there is plenty of water, lungfish live like normal fish. But in the dry season, their swamps and streams dry out. The lungfish have a special way of surviving. They dig burrows in the damp mud and curl up inside. Then they cover their bodies in slimy **mucus** to stop them drying out. They can stay like this for many months until it rains again.

LUNGFISH

BODY LENGTH:
UP TO 2 M (6.5 FT)

WEIGHT:
17 KG (37.4 LBS)

LIFESPAN:
10 YEARS (IN **CAPTIVITY**)

HABITAT:
SWAMPS AND STREAMS

THAT'S AMAZING!:
THE LUNGFISH BLOCKS THE ENTRANCE OF ITS BURROW WITH MUD. THE MUD KEEPS WATER OUT BUT LETS A SMALL AMOUNT OF AIR IN.

where lungfish live

Africa

Atlantic Ocean

Indian Ocean

Southern Ocean

Animals in danger

Many animals in Africa are in danger of dying out forever. When an animal dies out, it is said to be **extinct**. Animals are dying out because people are destroying their **habitats**, capturing them for pets, or killing them for their skins, meat, and body parts.

The black rhinoceros is in danger of becoming extinct. Tens of thousands of rhinos have been killed for their horns. Today, there are fewer than 4,000 black rhinos left, mainly living in East and South Africa. In West Africa, they may already be extinct.

Rhinos' horns are used to make dagger handles and some kinds of **traditional medicine**.

There are only about 360 of these mountain gorillas left in rainforests, in Central Africa.

Another animal at risk is the mountain gorilla. Many gorillas have been shot for food or killed in the wars taking place in the region. Others, especially babies, have been caught and taken away to be pets. The forest habitat where the gorillas live is also in danger of disappearing. Large areas of forest are being chopped down to make way for farms.

Today, **conservation** groups are working hard to save these amazing animals.

Animal facts and figures

There are millions of different kinds of animals living all over the world. The place where an animal lives is called its **habitat**. Animals have special features, such as wings, claws, and fins. These features allow animals to survive in their habitats. Which animal do you think is the most amazing?

SAVANNAH ELEPHANT

BODY LENGTH:
4–5 M (13–16 FT)

WEIGHT:
4–7 TONNES
(4.4–7.7 TONS)

LIFESPAN:
60 YEARS

HABITAT:
GRASSLAND

THAT'S AMAZING!:
AN ELEPHANT'S TUSKS GROW THROUGHOUT ITS LIFE AND CAN REACH MORE THAN 3 M (10 FT) LONG.

OSTRICH

HEIGHT:
1.7–2.7 M (5.7–8.8 FT)

WEIGHT:
UP TO 150 KG (330 LBS)

LIFESPAN:
50 YEARS

HABITAT:
GRASSLANDS; DESERTS

THAT'S AMAZING!:
OSTRICHES CAN LIVE WITHOUT WATER FOR A LONG TIME. THIS IS VERY USEFUL BECAUSE THEY LIVE IN DRY PLACES. THEY GET MOISTURE FROM THE PLANTS THEY EAT.

CHEETAH

BODY LENGTH:
UP TO 1.5 M (4.9 FT)

TAIL LENGTH:
UP TO 85 CM (33.1 IN)

WEIGHT:
40–65 KG (88–143 LBS)

LIFESPAN:
UP TO 12 YEARS

HABITAT:
GRASSLAND AND SEMI-DESERT

THAT'S AMAZING!:
CHEETAH CUBS SPEND MOST OF THEIR TIME PLAYING GAMES OF **STALKING** AND POUNCING. THIS IS A WAY OF PRACTISING FOR HUNTING WHEN THEY GROW UP.

GOLIATH BEETLE

BODY LENGTH:
UP TO 15 CM (5.8 IN)

WEIGHT:
70–100 G (2.4–3.5 OZ)

LIFESPAN:
FEW MONTHS (ADULTS)

HABITAT:
RAINFOREST

THAT'S AMAZING!:
GOLIATH BEETLES HAVE SHARP CLAWS AT THE END OF EACH LEG TO HELP THEM CLIMB TREES TO FEED.

GABOON VIPER

HEIGHT:
UP TO 2 M (6.56 FT)

WEIGHT:
7–10 KG (15–22 LBS)

LIFESPAN:
15–20 YEARS
(IN **CAPTIVITY**)

HABITAT:
RAINFOREST

THAT'S AMAZING!:
ONE GABOON VIPER
MAKES ENOUGH **VENOM**
TO KILL AT LEAST
50 MONKEYS.

AYE-AYE

HEIGHT:
30–40 CM (11.7–15.6 IN)

TAIL LENGTH:
40–50 CM (15.6–19.5 IN)

WEIGHT:
2–3 KG (4.4–6.6 LBS)

LIFESPAN:
UP TO 23 YEARS (IN
CAPTIVITY)

HABITAT:
RAINFORESTS, DRY
FORESTS IN MADAGASCAR

THAT'S AMAZING!:
THE AYE-AYE SPENDS THE
DAY SLEEPING IN A NEST
MADE FROM LEAVES AND
TWIGS, THEN GOES OUT
HUNTING AT NIGHT.

SOCIABLE WEAVERBIRD

BODY LENGTH:
14 CM (5.4 IN)

WEIGHT:
26–30 G (0.9–1 OZ)

LIFESPAN:
UP TO 5 YEARS

HABITAT:
DESERT

THAT'S AMAZING!:
A SOCIABLE WEAVERBIRD
NEST CAN WEIGH SEVERAL
TONNES. IT CAN GET SO
HEAVY THAT IT KNOCKS
DOWN THE TREE IT IS
BUILT ON.

DESERT LOCUST

BODY LENGTH:
4.5–6 CM (1.7–2.3 IN)

WEIGHT:
2 G (0.07 OZ)

LIFESPAN:
3–5 MONTHS

HABITAT:
DESERTS

THAT'S AMAZING!:
LOCUSTS LAY UP TO 100
EGGS IN AN EGG POD IN
THE SAND. THE FEMALE
COVERS THEM WITH
FOAMY FROTH TO STOP
THE EGGS DRYING OUT.

NILE CROCODILE

BODY LENGTH:
UP TO 6 M (19.6 FT)

WEIGHT:
225 KG (496 LBS)

LIFESPAN:
45 YEARS

HABITAT:
RIVERS, LAKES, **SWAMPS**

THAT'S AMAZING!:
CROCODILES SOMETIMES
HUNT IN GROUPS. THEY
HERD FISH TOWARDS THE
BANK, THEN EAT THEM!

LUNGFISH

BODY LENGTH:
UP TO 2 M (6.5 FT)

WEIGHT:
17 KG (37.4 LBS)

LIFESPAN:
10 YEARS (IN CAPTIVITY)

HABITAT:
SWAMPS AND STREAMS

THAT'S AMAZING!:
THE LUNGFISH BLOCKS
THE ENTRANCE OF ITS
BURROW WITH MUD.
THE MUD KEEPS WATER
OUT BUT LETS A SMALL
AMOUNT OF AIR IN.

Find out more

Books to read

Exploring Continents: Africa, Deborah Underwood (Heinemann Library, 2007)

Living Things: Adaptation, Holly Wallace (Heinemann Library, 2001)

Living Things: Survival and Change, Holly Wallace (Heinemann Library, 2001)

Websites

http://www.bbc.co.uk/nature/reallywild
Type in the name of the animal you want to learn about and find a page with lots of facts, figures, and pictures.

http://animals.nationalgeographic.com/animals
This site has information on the different groups of animals, stories of survival in different habitats, and stunning photo galleries to search through.

http://animaldiversity.ummz.umich.edu
A website run by the University of Michigan which has a huge encyclopedia of animals to search through.

http://www.mnh.si.edu
The website of the Smithsonian National Museum of Natural History, which has one of the largest natural history collections in the world.

Zoo sites
Many zoos around the world have their own websites which tell you about the animals they keep, where they come from, and how they are looked after.

Glossary

adapted when an animal has special features that help it to survive in its habitat

camouflage when an animal has special colours or markings which help to hide it in its habitat

captivity animals kept in a zoo or wildlife park live in captivity. Animals in captivity often live longer than wild animals because they have no predators, nor is there competition for food.

chamber area like a room

conservation saving and protecting threatened animals and habitats

continent one of seven huge pieces of land on Earth. Each continent is divided into smaller regions called countries.

equator imaginary line running around the middle of the Earth

extinct when a kind of animal dies out forever

gill part of a fish's body which is used for breathing in the water

grassland huge, open space covered in grass and bushes

habitat place where an animal lives and feeds

insect animal with six legs and three parts to its body

larvae grub-like young of insects

mammal animal that has fur or hair and feeds its babies on milk

mate when an animal makes babies with another animal

mucus thick, slimy liquid

prey animals that are hunted and killed by other animals for food

rainforest thick forest growing around the Equator where the weather is hot and wet

reptile animal with scaly skin that lays eggs on land

stalk move by creeping quietly

swamp area where large parts of the land are usually or always under water

swarm huge group of animals, such as insects

traditional medicine old-fashioned kind of medicine

tropical places around the equator which are hot and wet all year round

venom another word for poison

Index